Rain Falling by the River

Rain Falling by the River

new and selected poems of the spirit

Christopher Southgate

CANTERBURY
PRESS
Norwich

© Christopher Southgate 2017

First published in 2017 by the Canterbury Press Norwich
Editorial office
3rd Floor, Invicta House
108–114 Golden Lane
London EC1Y 0TG, UK

Canterbury Press is an imprint of Hymns Ancient & Modern Ltd
(a registered charity)

Hymns Ancient & Modern® is a registered trademark of
Hymns Ancient & Modern Ltd
13A Hellesdon Park Road, Norwich,
Norfolk NR6 5DR, UK

www.canterburypress.co.uk

British Library Cataloguing in Publication data

A catalogue record for this book is available
from the British Library

978 1 84825 968 3

Typeset by Regent Typesetting
Printed and bound in Great Britain by
CPI Group (UK) Ltd, Croydon

Contents

Part Three   Explorations of Place

Part Four   Songs of Suffering

We have to become as simple and as wordless as the growing corn or the falling rain.

Etty Hillesum

Introduction

This collection draws together published work from the last thirty years with new unpublished poems. During those years I have been a house-husband, a bookseller, a lay chaplain – first in a university and then on mental health wards in a major hospital – a teacher of theology, and a puzzler-away at God. With my infinitely dear and long-suffering wife Sandy I have also offered and promoted lay ministry in the little village churches where we live on the edge of Dartmoor.

The poems all deal more or less explicitly with spiritual themes. They range from the straightforwardly devotional, such as 'Compline', to the politically prophetic, such as 'The Unit', and the mystically reflective, such as the musings on the experience of prayer in 'River'. There are also wry responses to famous texts, as in 'The Fall' and 'Self-appraisal of a Mage'.

The book is in five parts. The first marks out the territory of spiritual exploration for the whole book, beginning with my commissioned poem for the 400th anniversary of the King James translation. I was greatly honoured when Rowan Williams quoted the poem in his sermon at the Westminster Abbey service in honour of the anniversary on 16 November 2011.[1]

Part Two consists of poems on biblical themes, often taking the part of a biblical character, or bringing someone into focus whom the text depicts at the edge of the scene, like Matthias, the substitute apostle chosen by lot. King David appears, and

Job, and Mary Magdalene, but always the focus of the section is drawn back to the figure of Jesus.

Part Three contains poems on place – great places of spiritual tradition, such as Patmos, Iona and Lindisfarne, and places that have struck me very forcibly, like Yosemite Valley and the site of 9/11 in New York.

Part Four consists of poems directly inspired by meditation on death, bereavement and suffering. It includes 'Coming to Terms', which has been a help to many trying to find words for their situation of loss. Also here are poems deriving from profound encounters on psychiatric wards.

Finally, Part Five comprises my own spiritual responses to various catalysts – situations in my life, but also works of art, poetry and music. The motif of prayer in all its mystery is threaded through the whole collection, and is where the book ends.

---

1 Archbishop Rowan's quote from the first poem in the book was:

To begin on the Bible
To be caught by the rise of a huge wave breaking
To know all the conflict and chaos to be faced
If their book could not command
The nation, the language, in a foment of becoming.
They heard Scripture's ancient voices, remote,
Tasting of the desert,
Its longing, in a strange land.
Their task they called
A paradise of trees of life. Long hard years
They walked in this forest.

He ended his sermon: 'So we listen in turn; and we walk into that forest, among the trees of life.'

The book is dedicated with great gratitude to staff and students of the South West Ministry Training Course, for thirty years of forest-walking, and for much fellowship and challenge and friendship.

PART ONE

Points of Departure

Rendering Voices

a poem for the 400th anniversary of the King James Bible

To begin on the Bible
To be caught by the rise of a huge wave breaking
To know all the conflict and chaos to be faced
If their book could not command
The nation, the language, in a foment of becoming.
They heard Scripture's ancient voices, remote,
Tasting of the desert,
Its longing, in a strange land.

Their task they called
A paradise of trees of life. Long hard years
They walked in this forest,
Dividing it into six sections,
Into exercise books, trading
Sigla and suggestions in rooms
Where kings had died and disciplines
Had been invented.

They threw strained eyes up at ceilings
Of hammer-beams, at gilt stars.
Every section was read aloud, the company
Some with eyes closed, some stroking pomaded beards,
Listening like poets at a workshop
For a false footfall, for any hint
Of ugliness. Only the words that formed
Like birds in the mouth, only they survived.

The ancient voices still arrive out of the past
Like a time capsule. They are smuggled
Into harsh places. They are raked over
On revisionist laptops. We bring to them
Immense science, but less confidence
That our words, put to the anvil, rubbed and polished
By the right number of learned men
Will last, or that they should.

Still the wave breaks over us
Shifting us in our chaos
Still it makes, in every age and tongue,
Insistent claims

In the beginning God
                The Lord is my shepherd
Vanity of vanities
                We beheld his glory
The glory as of the only begotten of the Father
Full of grace and truth.

My copy, given to me at three months old, is inscribed
In my godmother's hand. I treasure it. In student essays
I insist on the NRSV.
I download parables from *The Message*,
                      preach on them,
But it is the words that survived the tyrannous scrutiny
Of the beard-stroking poets, the birds in the mouth,
The words given me as a young child
That I will hear in my head when I am dying.

Dedicated to my godmother Barbara William-Olsson (1921–2010), who gave me my first copy of the King James Bible. Love suffers long, and is kind.

River

On the Sabbath day we went out of the gate by the river,
where we thought there would be a place of prayer.

Acts 16.13

We found a bright pool
The light almost too hard to look upon
And rested there awhile.

We found a quick place
Where the driving water
Made arrows of foam.

Later, a long slow brown slide
Under great trees.
We saw ourselves sharp in reflection

Until suddenly we were in a great torrent
A place of such buffeting
That our spirits were thrashed upside down, whirled sideways,

Spat out from there, washing up
On an island of old stone.
Not knowing the place, but feeling somehow known,
All the time wondering.

Compline

Into thy hands
I commend my spirit.
It fits in them
Exactly.

What if

What if we were only our work?
>   relentless appraisal, specious promotion,
>   inexorable redundancy
>   or edged-out retirement.

What if we were only our illnesses?
>   A mass of scans, bilirubin levels, cytokines.
>   We exchange parameters,
>   scans of masses.

What if we were only our loves?
>   only the times with the ones
>   we have been naked beside
>   or held, desperately, in the night?

What if in this tremendous darkness
>   there were no stars
>   or they incited
>   no wonder.

What if we were never as little children?

Grey Epiphany, Hungerford Bridge

Across the steel coloured water
every humour of humanity passes.
Christmas negotiated, and the sales,
there is a moment at sunset that seems suddenly full of love,
of heart-lift. People touch,
they open their hips and smile
they anoint the air of the bridge
with kisses, and laughter.
The Ecuadorian band grin
and riff with new intensity
against the clacking of the trains.
The moment passes. Kids are grumpy,
roller-skate into each other. Collars
are turned. The evening city
crouches in on itself
in a brittle, man-made light.
I try not to evaluate
the currency of moments.
They come as useless gifts
like gold to a newborn.

Arvo Pärt's 'Psalom' by Last Firelight

Notes trying for phrases, trying for purpose
on a river of silence.
The cats' ears pricked, shifting
at tonalities. My eyes fixed
on embers. A high violin
stretches out notes,
questioning, praying.

The last coals are distinct now,
each glow surging from end to end
as if searching for a way
to perpetuate itself, then
subsiding into greyness.
The cats like statues of themselves
watch for the moment
when they'll become invisible.
Notes strain for silence.

Impressions of Faith

(my faith), which was never strong, is being beaten into mere
gold leaf, and flutters in weak rags from the letter of its old
forms.

Ruskin, writing to Henry Acland

Cracked, broken icons,
gold surfaces
dull and fading.

Gold leaf, atoms thin,
lacks all mechanical strength,
focusses X-rays.

Three things, then, remain:
a flutter of beaten gold,
slender hope, fierce love.

Chaplain's Sonnet

for K. H.

Speaking of God. Speaking without answers.
Stretching slippery words into the suicide
Of a girl for want of beta-blockers.
Postulating a rock in a bad tide
Racing to ebb.   Shake the grieving hands.
Feel a solidarity that calls not
On the name of God, defiantly bands
Together, accepts its bitter lot.

Live out the God-job. Call clangingly
For access of joy, and feel on your face
Friends' scepticism, stingingly.
God-words, they say, have lost their place.
Whatever is true and good, they say, think you
On those things. Reach always for the true.

This also is not Thou

Cadence

A star
becomes a star
becomes a leaf
eaten by a worm
which becomes a being
who can cast eyes heavenward
and say
There is no God.

Communiqué

I am not this or that
Rather I am pure other.

I do not desire the blood of bulls
I weep no tears over that pap.

Purity of heart interests me

When there is darkness over the land
You see and do not see me.

Riddle

Man.
Fish.
First fruit.

Unicorn.
Pelican.
Second of Three.

Word Man.
Hanged Man.

In Memoriam *R. S. Thomas*

Your verse, a house of potent viruses –
Calvary, Kierkegaard, Prytherch –

Infected us, not with faith,
But with acceptance of a space of in-between,

A mountain-land where faith and doubt
Inhabit each other's shadow.

Your death leaves us still on the lower slopes,
Bereft of a good guide.

Palimpsest – a prayer

I have been in your in-tray all my life
Though I did not know it
And thought I wrote
My own itinerary
In my own alphabet
On the rough, second-grade vellum
You had provided.

I cannot read those old destinations
Now – nor have I love enough
To regret them. I can only peer
Into the bare, summary logia
Running from future to past across
My much-corrupted palimpsest.
Your Aramaic style is good, although
They say you could not write,
And knew no Greek,
And told good stories,
Lived and died them.

Hold up the parchment, Lord,
Scrape the surface clean.
It is scored through and through
With failed love for virtue,
Obscuring the Kingdom's character-set.
Inscribe me a song to sing –
And give me the prodigal's part;
I know by heart the song
Of the other brother.

Write in light, Lord,
That I may still read
When my blood cools,
Still remember
When my song fails,
Still catch sight of you
When I sit to write,
Or share
In breaking bread.

PART TWO

From the Bible

The Fall

They'd been there for years, of course,
Hugging trees, logging the animals by name,
Taking afternoon tea with the Lord God –
Occasionally He would stay for spritzers.

They were pretty cool, those gatherings
In the cool of the day,
But well, you know, things happen ...

One day when Adam was classifying arachnids
Eve began to coil her imagination around a certain serpent –
Virtual, of course, but so green
It made the green mamba look pale,

So sinuous it made her screen blur before her eyes
And you can guess the rest.

She went ahead and clicked on a new icon –
It was the one on which God had said
She shouldst on no account click.

At once she was offered
A free holiday. She called Adam over
And they interfaced as never before.

Then they looked at each other, and knew
That what they'd been doing till then
Was not just living, as they'd thought.
It had been *a lifestyle choice*.

All too short a step from there
To making bad ones.

Exile

In Babylon, everything came clear
Sitting by the fountains and ziggurats,
Tending the gardens of the oppressor
Nights crammed into garrets
Or harems. Watching the foreigners' pomp,
Its meticulous infrastructure,
They understood their sin, the slump
In their vision. They had traded their future
For surfaces, slaked their need for prayer
With style and footballers' wives.
In the gardens they saw the desert's glory –
They saw the rigour of lives
Stretched out at the feet of the Lord.
They heard the Babylon-encompassing hugeness of his song,
Hard, cosmic, brooding, and they sang.

David, Bathsheba and Jonathan

I had had various wives, by then,
aware only in myself of a proper kingly appetite,
and a huge yearning for the sound of his voice
that day he shot arrows, and I hid in the stone-heap.

Then I saw from the palace window someone content
in herself, in her own beauty, as he had been.
I saw it in the angle of her back
as she oiled herself on her rooftop, singing.

To get her I did evil, deserved and hated the prophet's
chill impeachment. I longed for straightness of love.

David and Abishag the Shunammite

No, do not rise yet, dark one, last love.
Leave your brown limbs around me
a moment longer. A king's bones grow very cold.
A king's sagged flesh ... which was taut as sling-cord ...
grows sour and rots before your puzzled eyes.

Once, I would have wrapped you in vine-leaves,
and licked honey off each soft shoulder, olive breast.
But a king's bones ... At night your hands frame my face
before your last kiss. Are you counting the days
of your safety? A king, still. Do not rise yet, Shunammite.

The Statement of Job's Comforters

Our training had prepared us.
We were conversant with the chasm
that separates sufferer from comfort –
the land of loose stone, broken hope,
the bridges silence lays.

The Temanitic School of Analytic Theology
had suggested to us the extent
of defences that might be encountered.
We worked both together and separately.
It was agreed that fees be waived.

In retrospect we can only deplore
the intervention of the Lord God –
who lacked external accreditation,
had no supervisor, and had the gall
to question *our* methods.

Madonna and Child

from 'Transcriptions' – a series of drawings by Dennis Creffield

Madonna, and the swaddled child on the angle
Of her arm, are one shape, an icon
Of wholeness. The mother, a young Semitic
Girl, wears black, her tenderness already
Includes mourning. The child stirs.

                                              The angles
                              Of the icon
                  Of the mother
                      In black
Are those of Pietà.

                              The child
On her arm
Is wholeness.
                  He receives our tenderness
                                      Impatiently.

Madonna
            Arms clasping.
                                      A young Semitic
Girl, shy, frightened.
                      The child comforting her.

                  Swaddled
      We can talk of unions –
The Earth as great Mother –
                  May the darkness of God
                      Make us stir,

Proclaim the love the child has been to us.

Three Deserted Wives

after T. S. Eliot's 'Journey of the Magi'

A cold coming they had of it, we heard,
And were glad. We'd not been consulted,
But it gave us a chance to deal
With the silken girls.
For the first time to know
Equal meeting.

We learned the flute together,
Sat in a triangle of tents,
Complacent with shapelessness, swayed
By songs of bitter queens.
In succession of days
There was healing.

We learned that a graceful circle
Was pleasing in its own right.
We danced gravely, sweeping
Shawls to the Mother of all.
In growth of new incense-trees
There was power.

Wizened women of the country
Were our diviners. The old questions
Could be safely disregarded,
Weeds in our well-tended garden.
At night we danced wild,
Each a different creature.

The earthquake in the north mountains
Laid flat the new plain palaces
Where we had sought to centre,
Scattered camels, beat at faith.
Stereotyped, we nursed
Resented wounded.

They returned at last, bringing us
No presents. They spoke of birth,
Which we had given them, and death –
Already heavy on the ochre air.
Questions of lordship hummed
On northern hills.

Our flutes are cracked now, and played
Only to chide children. We meet
At night, begin to understand
Their talk of brokenness.

Self-appraisal of a Mage

Principal achievement during the appraisal period?
> Difficult journey in winter.

Punctuality?
> Just in time.

Main difficulties experienced?
> Lazy and corrupt camel-drivers.

Disappointments?
> Not enough sherbet.

Self-assessment of performance?
> Satisfactory.

Best relationship with work colleague?
> Balthasar, a balm to my soul.

Most problematic relationship?
> Melchior. Argues back.

Information provided for the furtherance of your work?
> None.

Future developmental aspirations?
> Being part of a death.

Interview with Nicodemus

There are a good many signs and wonders
These days. I have not gone in
For that sort of thing very much.
There are others who delight in deciphering
The tricks of magicians, and the protestations
Of would-be deliverers.
It has been enough for me to know
God's Law, and to teach it
And to do the relevant committee work.

I begin with that statement – yes
It is important to set something down;
The record depends on it. We annotate
What God gave us long ago.

I thought he was a man who deserved
A fair hearing. By night, yes
But not like a terrorist or a thief.
Simply a man prudent of his colleagues.

It went as badly, and as well
As I could possibly have imagined.
What is this theology we play at? A game
For children? I came away a child.

I can tell you exactly. I memorised it
Though it kept slipping away as I hurried
Back through streets elusive with shadow.
In the end I wrote it down
In Hebrew and Latin and Greek,
The three languages of significance to God,
And hid the tablet in an old well
In my garden

If it is ever found I will be a martyr
Or a hero, unsatisfactory roles for a teacher
Of the Law. There is one phrase
That stays with me always.
It is the colour of the night in those streets
And the sound of my heart pumping:
It has about it a dangerous tang of joy, and
He spoke it as though he were the wind himself.

When I feel myself dying I will teach it
At the Gate of Beauty – Gamaliel,
If he is alive, will save me a lynching.
'The Spirit blows where it wills. You hear
The sound of it, but you do not know where
It comes from, or where it is going.
So with everyone who is born of spirit.'

I digress. We have talked enough.
I have nothing to say.
I watch and I wait.

The Upper Room

from the tree-trunk sculpture of that name by Colin Wilbourn
on the riverbank below Durham Cathedral

The river hauls itself round a slow
Corner, a mud-coloured plate on which
Reflections soften into laminar flow.
And that is time, gathering itself, time
Gathers quite slowly towards Jerusalem.

Durham offers many parables – the fortress
Church, the dark recesses of God
Into which dead saints are gathered.
And this household of shaved elms
By the river. The feast is quite simple –

Here are the vessels we each are, part-
Carved, sharing solidity with neighbours.
Rivalry of height is mocked by his
Sturdy sitting. On his left is Judas –
No vessel, but a window – through him

Every gale beyond Eden blows.
The world's weight gathers massive
Upon a felled tree – time quickens
To a roar, drowning
Strange words of blessing.

After towel and pitcher time will be flung
To a climax. This is the house of now,
Ceasing to exist as the eleven leave,
The Master leading them,
And they sing their hearts away.

Pentimento

Change of mind is said to be a good test
of authenticity. The painterly
intelligence plays, risks – uncertainty
is alien to the copyist.

In Gethsemane we note the hesitation.
It helps us see
the authenticity, the humanness.

But for the subject himself
leaving his friends exhausted and sleeping
this was the hateful test.

Would not a consummate forger
impart pentimento to deceive?
Surely at this of all moments

he should be confident of the composition?

It was the mob, coming in from the right,
Iscariot leading,
that reassured him.

Dark Relief

I come on to kill the mood
if there's any jollity about
or even worse, hint of joy.

In my time I've blighted Chaplin and Cleese
mocked Socrates and ridiculed the Buddha,
seen zits on the face of Helen of Troy.

I had trouble only with the Nazarene.
He had that gift that some – a few – have
of making others feel better about the world.

But in his case it lasted – they stayed changed –
his own shoulders slumped a fraction more each time
but the sodding woman at the well, and fucking Zacchaeus,

I've heard the stories
too many times.
They stayed changed.

I saw him towards the end
the weight of the cross on his back
seeming to fit somehow. Seeming to complete him.

There passed between us
I remember
a look of total understanding.

He took in my hatred of all delight.
He saw my inescapable calling
and I saw his.

I come on to kill the mood.
It's what I do.
But without savour,

without zest, pride in my work,
since that day
in ugly, fetid old Jerusalem
the mood too dark to kill.

The Cup

I played my part.
I am heavy two-handled Roman silver.
I am used for wine, volcanic wine of Orvieto,
Apulian red. Rot-gut Palestinian stuff
all resins and tannins
when the Procurator's steward forgets.

I was filled with water that day
pumped up from the Gihon
through that old tunnel – some long-dead king's –
chill and clear
drawn from the life-blood of the city.
And the Procurator washed his hands.

My surface reflected his face,
narrowed eyes,
terse lips, frown.
He flung the beads of water
not at the prisoner
but at the waiting crowd.

Other things happened that day.
There was a thunderstorm towards evening
clearing the air, replenishing the aquifers.
It was cold again that night;
they lit the brazier again
in the courtyard.

Tears were cried into me that night.
Tears of pointless scruple – his wife's,
wept into a good sweet Samian.
I am a Roman cup
robust, two-handled,
made for stronger stuff than tears.

Gifts

First let it be clear – no gift is simple. For our part
We offered a nuanced disaffection
Well-versed in the French theorists.

In a ludic nod at tradition
We brought gold, in an ebony casket,
Little gilt line-cutters, and a useful box.

We brought incense in silver-studded teak
For the long swing of thurible,
The rise of ritual towards unknowing.

We brought myrrh in alabaster.
We made a significant investment
In the equipment of lamentation.

And we were there
So others said
When it counted.

We had brought texts, and a fine air-nozzle
Wonderful for cleaning celluloid
And dusting the pollen from lilies.

We waited thirty years.

And in return? Only his dereliction.
The obscenity
Of his forgiveness.

Magdalene in the Garden

'If it is you, Sir, who have removed
him, tell me where you have laid him, and I'll
take him away. An end to this affair.
    Tell me where you have laid him.
Please. If only you will give him to me
we shall be alone together once –
there were always others, endless cares.
    Tell me where you have laid him.
And Judas always feared the chance of scandal –
as though there could be greater shame, than that
such a man should wring out his end, bared
    Tell me where you have laid him.
under Pilate's placard. John was wary too –
jealous, I'd say, though seeing him with Mary
yesterday – well – an end to envy's snare.
    Tell me where you have laid him.
Strange, we all thought more of each other yesterday,
weeping, waiting for soldiers to come,
remembering the freedom of the road, where
    Tell me where you have laid him.
we were so often hungry, dusty,
triumphant. Wondering if they'd move on Shabbat.
Those early days, you know, I did not dare
    Tell me where you have laid him.
look anywhere but his feet. A strong walker.
Loved the extra league, the tendons' stretch,
and I, too, loved it, beating out air,
    Tell me where you have laid him.

staying with him, though he'd always pick
out a slow one, strengthen up their stride,
I did not have him to myself, anywhere.
      Tell me where you have laid him.
How thoughts wander now – Shabbat on the road,
its unearthly peace, our lostness to all
but God – we'd nothing, but when he'd tear
      Tell me where you have laid him.
a loaf it was enough, it was life to us.
Tell me, and I, scorned for what I was, saved
by love alone, bitter as myrrh, will bear
      Tell me where you have laid him.
the cursed corpse away for last farewell,
asking the dead eyes guidance, giving
the dear mouth words ... Why do you stare?
      Tell me where you have laid him.
Only give him to me, and I will drench
the dead feet with nard, and wipe them with my hair.'

'Ma-ry.'

Saul at the Stoning of Stephen

A man was roasting nuts at a brazier.
Closer to the gate, Saul stood
With the pile of cloaks. There was one
He liked the look of, yellow stars
Woven seamless into the fabric.

He had never seen a stoning
And had thought the missiles
Would be small, hurled from a distance.
This was up close and personal,
With boulders, discarded building blocks,

The stones themselves shouting
Condemnation. There was an ugly
Blood-lust to it – he made a note
That this was to be avoided.
What had to be done

Should be done with sorrow.
He looked away at the end –
Missed the man's dying prayer.
There was an odd light – he forced himself
To focus on it – like a wound in the sky

Somewhere to the north-east.

The lot fell on Matthias

at the beginning of the Acts of the Apostles (Acts 1.21–26),
Christ's disciples chose a successor to Judas Iscariot, drawing
lots between two candidates

I was not at all sure I wanted it.
Judas' seat, that is.
Even as they talked it through
I could see the confusion in the group.
Choosing a twelfth seemed like superstition.

Besides, I sensed trouble ahead. I did not fear
the priests, as much as Pharisees
who would suddenly see the light
and come in knowing it all
and wanting to change everything.

I did not want it – a seat in all that contestation.
I sang the Psalms with them, broke bread,
balanced the books, kept my counsel.
In material things we held all in common –
an accountant's nightmare.

I missed most his voice.
How he laughed at me.
How he looked into my heart.
He knew, and never told anyone,
about that first day on the lakeshore.

It rained hard that day (no-one
mentions that). Raindrops bounced off the lake,
glinted as they fell. Then in the sudden
sunlight he was standing there,
robe soaked, bantering with the brothers.

I listened by a rickety shed
smelling of fish. The voice changed,
began to talk of fishing for men
and I ducked into that stinking shed.
He saw me do it.

I would never have taken Judas' seat
but for those minutes, cowering in that shed,
before I bundled my fear into my bag
and ran up the hill towards glory.

The Unit

new anti-terrorist measures in Britain call for a process of 'compulsory deradicalisation'

I remember the rabbi. He was from nowhere much.
But not a man we could easily forget.
The session started well enough. He agreed
To the justice of the payment of fair taxes.
                                        Blessed,
He said, *are the peacemakers.*
This was promising. I marked it on his chart.

His voice was extraordinary. It was just as well
There were six of us on shift
Including some of our toughest. One of us
Had even heard Richard Dawkins in the flesh.
                                        Blessed
Are the pure in heart, the rabbi said, like sunlight
Beyond a storm, lighting up a distant sea.

This wasn't going in a good direction.
I looked around for help.
                                        Blessed,
He insisted, *are those who hunger and thirst*
After righteousness. It was like the first kiss
I ever shyly received
From the first woman I truly loved. *They shall be filled.*

We read him the sharpest chapter of *The God Delusion.*
We water-boarded him, just once or twice.
Four is the maximum quota on the Unit.

Blessed

(again, again) *are the meek.*
They shall inherit the earth. We even tried
The Church's concealment of abuse.

After that he seemed reluctant to say more
But we made him, as we do.
So quietly I could hardly hear.

Blessed

Are the poor in spirit. And looking
Me straight in the eye, missing two front teeth now,
Those who know their need of God.

At Toledo, once, before the *auto-da-fé*
The prisoner was released
Without full deradicalisation.
Most of us were not minded
To repeat the mistake.

The last stanza derives from Dostoevsky's myth of Christ appearing before the Grand Inquisitor in The Brothers Karamazov.

PART THREE

Explorations of Place

Patmos

There is only ever our own fear, our own desire
Warring in our heavens, wherever we
Try to escape ourselves, wherever the fire
Of sunrise meets us. Thus runs the theory.
So even John, on wind-weary Patmos,
Caught in the cosmic symphony of his vision,
Argued bitterly with his Ephesus
Self, and fretted at his former friends' derision.

We may feel along the cavern floor for John's
Finger-holds, or sing our praises on the beach,
Or haunt some ouzo place, flaunting our tans.
It does not change the silver of which each
Is made. But we can be woven by such a place,
Or spun, or twisted, in this brief time of grace.

Iona

I come six hundred miles to be here –
exchange heather for heather, Dartmoor streams
for Sound of Mull. I come for sorting,
space, aloneness. I am content
when the mist falls
                              on Scotland to the east.

For centuries they used this place to bury kings.
Then it lay forgotten, island
among many of the Lords of Argyll.
The ferry now crosses, recrosses
as thousands come
                              to borrow misty peace.

How Columba would have wondered,
standing by his wattle cell, staring
into Scotland, the Christless hills.
This island of burial, memory, retreat
danced under his feet
                              like a springboard.

Lindisfarne

I How Aidan and his monks came to Lindisfarne

They saw the setting sun cast a gleam
Over low, sea-hugging cliffs of Farne.

They chose a windblown rock, mimicked
Blessed Iona. They built in oak.

They saw how play of sea-otters bettered
Joy. They bound to them the Trinity.

They chose simple ways, the Master's, fishing
For pagan souls. They spelled out Gospels.

They saw dark stones of their new shore baptised
By seeping tide, day on day, and still black.

They chose the gyring wind, harshness of Farne,
Joy. They bound to them the Trinity.

II Coming to Lindisfarne

Early onto the windblown flats
to find the light
already gone from Farne
and on the holy island
church on church knocked down.
The wind whispers urgently
to the sand. The island
seems to shiver.
The sand whips in fast whispers
away across the beach
into the swallowing sea.

49

Cuthbert used to stand all night
waist-deep in water, praying.
I shall never know
that continuity of sea and flesh –
otters' acceptance,
gift of cormorant's fish –
but sense, from the wind on the stone,
how those early prayers hang stubborn
about the scattered Farne,
and bind unto myself, this day,
the threefold God of sea and sky.

Manhattan

Return to Ground Zero, 2012

No entry to the new memorial.
On-line booking is down
                        because of the hurricane.
I lose my chance to lose my eyes
in a square pool inside a square pool
in water falling out of falling.

Instead I sit in a small church;
a choir grapples with Bach
                        in a place
where firemen slept on pews,
and on boards and railings there gathered
line on line of pleas for the missing
lines about the missing.

The conductor tells the choir
                        they are all over the place.
Which is what here is, eleven years on.
It will not settle into history, this jumble
of mementoes, teddy bears,
badges from fire departments across the world –
outstretched longing, letters left about longing.

Eleven years ago I looked down at Ground Zero
                              still burning.
Relatives were being led in to breathe
the ruined, lachrymal air.
I am not able to drown that memory
                              in neat square pools;
on-line booking is down, because of the hurricane.
There is only this jumbled hoping, this endlessly battered
    hoping about loving.

Amsterdam

The Beguinehof

A cast of a woman praying. She was taught
by prayer. She was taught by Eckhart.
She was always an object of suspicion,
finding and giving refuge. Amsterdam
buys and sells, burns blithe around her.

The air of the courtyard
seems drawn into laminar flow, ordered
by the offices of prayer.
The quiet of it is the quiet under the canopy
of a deep forest in winter – the spirit of each Beguine

like a reaching tree,
sheltering.

Rhodes

Houses of Bread

A tiny red-tiled church.
Groins of veined stone hold an apse
which frames an altar. A candle
floating in a cup of water
flickers out its flame.

In Ottoman times this place
became the bakery for the Muslim poor.
Its chimney survives as a window.
The walls remember their service –
leaven and ash.

On the beach there is a bakery,
a kind of concrete shack
where a family turns out
crusty caraway-grained loaves, the locals'
daily sustenance.

The place sweats heat
catches the salt-spray
fuses it with woodsmoke, cinnamon,
patience, caraway,
ash and leaven.

Montpellier: Cathédrale St Pierre

The limbs of oaks make an intricate lattice
through which cathedral towers shine.
A blackbird sings an Occitanic blackbird song.
The towers lean their weight
on two massive cylinders of stone,
float above them, sentinel,
playing with the evening sunlight.
Their task is to praise
to be admired
to strike the hours to eternity.
They leave the hard geometry to the trees.

St Guilhem-le-Désert: Cloister

On the hills above
ruined towers of hermits.

In a small rectangular pool
a few carp.

A simple garden
given over to herbs.

At the lavender flowers, a butterfly, then two
negotiate the hot breeze.

Cricket-song serrates
thousand-year-old quiet.

Torcello

Looking East

They like bricks here.
The path from the vaporetto is herringboned brick.
You walk this neat pilgrim way
As far as the basilica, which raises plain brick walls
Straight up toward heaven.
You may escape here with your learning and your current
    gospel:
The walls, unadorned, aloof on their columns
Tell you this is all straw.

The bishop of the place was elevated, via steep brick steps
So he might stare the better
At the stark laddered crucifix
                    And beyond it, the Last Judgement.
Only the Virgin, vast in black on a pale gold ground,
Contemplates this vision with serenity.
The walls tell you: sit quiet – in the humblest place –
Until you feel the Judgement is behind you.

Mozambique

Rosetta

from the flooding in early 2000. Media pictures included a
woman who had given birth to her baby in a tree

We lost sight of Sophia
In some parking-lot or other;
The wisdom to plan for the next generation
Deserted us – or we abandoned her
For reminding us
Of free-market failure.

To attract our attention
Sophia has to lie sprawled in a tree
While the stream she was born by
Hurls below her,
Swollen, twisting,
Junk-strewn, body-strewn.

In her moment in the news
Sophia gives birth – not to the anointed one
But to one more peasant baby for the millennium –
Rosetta. Born in a tree.
Fragility among thorns.
Daughter of wisdom.

Let it not take three thousand years
For us to decipher her.

Mission Santa Clara, California

At mass, on the thirteenth Sunday of ordinary time,
I find myself weeping for no reason I know.
I walk out into a strew of jacaranda flowers
Like pale shreds of a purple cloak.

The garden is quietness, and placed light.
They lost eight from here, in El Salvador,
Gunned down by the Government.

Ignatius in bronze reads his Exercises
To a fountain of struck rock, to oaks, catalpas,
Olive trees from the days when this was Spain.

A chopper heads out for the coast.
Jacaranda leaves, delicate as the flight-feathers
Of a hawk, notice the breeze.

What does one remember,
In the moment of martyrdom?
What place, what curve of love, what wave breaking?

What can I even begin to feel
Protected by the Patriot Act
And the searching of my shoes at every airport?

The trees of the garden,
Having taken breath, reply: wait –
Wait till Ignatius turns the page.

Yosemite Valley

I from Washburn Point

Mile and mile and mile of pines,
the ground hidden, always rising.
Finally a vista which,
so much looked for, now appals.
The glacier-track is a sick gleam
of exposed, raked rock,
like work still in the studio
of some macabre sculptor.
I have longed to see this
yet want to declare it
unfinished, not ready
for its public, till trees are born
on the scars, and the cliff faces
heal.

II from the Merced River

The valley is a tunnel of lighting effects:
ivories on Half-Dome, while other
cliffs, Eumenides, wait
in grave-grey silence
to have their say.
On mountain faces
the strivings of unproved braves
climbing amid the weaving swifts,
and old profiles, like Titian's
self-portrait at ninety.

Evening comes, and morning,
and these hills are there to be sought,
to change me, as they themselves
change.

III *retrospect*

A way-station of the imagination
between the High Sierra
and the sea. A snapshot
of rock-cutting fate. And if
it be true, and I believe it,
Nature sings of her creator,
Yosemite then's a cradle of this praise.

PART FOUR

Songs of Suffering

Funeral Films

to understand bereavement
we must first come to terms
with our own deaths.

from a training session on death and dying

I have a clear picture of my own
Funeral. Threatened rain has held off;
The light is limpid, photographic,
The church four-square, full, every pew
Taken, but the churchwardens cope.

The sermon is brief and to the point.
A cello suite is played without flaw.
There are many tributes, even from
Those I hardly knew, and mourners
Weep decorously at the graveside.

My film of *her* service is blurred –
I know that short, brisk, Crem. formula,
But I do not hear it, or notice
When it ends. My life's shutter is jammed.
Anger churns inside me, anger at her –
I would rather stay angry than
Be alone. I taste that death's dry swallowing
And seize hold of the anger;
Endlessly I play it back at God –
I cannot see, I cannot see why

There will not always be this cleanness,
This brilliance of late breakfasts, coffee
Smells, and Scarlatti, and oranges,
And Lapsang-coloured shadows on silk
And cheesecloth, and port-coloured shadows
In evenings of light remembering.
Instead bedpans, vomiting, incontinence,
Sedations, sad layings-on of hands,
Instructions unheard, incoherent,
The sudden nearness of God, and dark.

And so when the session is over
I fix up tennis, plan holidays
For the year after next, hold her
Tighter than need be. I leave both films
To fog in the light of prayer. As Saint Teresa
Says, we must open every door
In the mansion, and let love in.

I pray
To be the one left. I pray
Never to be left.

Coming to Terms

Where are these terms
they are telling me
I must come to?

What they are saying to me
is that I am not as they are
(they thank their God)

But I could be – will be –
when I have come –
as they put it – to terms.

I nod my head
I do not say
(for this would make them uncomfortable)

that terms is a place
I do not want to come to
for that would be to say

that you are gone
that this colour of sky
the streets at evening

empty, endlessly walked,
this sound of dawn
this scent of waking alone

are the real colours, sounds,
scents of things,
without you there.

That my dream
in which you lie by my side

and tell me again of your love
and kiss my heart better
is a dream.

Terms is a place
of present tenses
laboriously corrected to past.

It is down a long tunnel –
once in there I might lose sight
of the lines of your face.

Coming to terms would mean accepting
that others have felt this before
and will again,

that these conversations
in which I tell you everything
are only one-way.

Terms might even be a place
where I had parted with your clothes
packed up your books, your music.

Terms is a far-off country.
It lies beyond
many stilted storytellings.

I do not choose
to come there.

Crows at a Funeral

Wheeling under laden, pall-coloured cloud
The carrion birds. Seeing them yaw and pitch
And corkscrew across the storm, the day we all
Went to bury Helen, I could not help
Admire persistence in the *Corvidae*.

They're up in all conditions, and though
We scan the sky for more uplifting symbols
The crows are compulsory. Fair-weather
Soaring hawks, planing ease, are like
The life of adverts for Pernod and jeans –

Lazy, effortless, taloned, and rapacious.
These black banalities mob our soarings,
Turning too quickly outside our grasp,
Slipping away from reprisal, raucously calling
'Decay, decay, and death that gives us life'.

This teeming day, full of tears and weather,
Holds little for hedonists. A caucus of crows
Blusters through our consciousness. We talk
Raucously of resurrections. The certainty
Is deposited in the over-full churchyard.

Our hope, beyond the bitter wind, is in
The Word that made the ravens, arrayed lilies,
Cast crows as reality. Who suffered
To make sense for us of loss, and service,
And of this so sullen, leering, anvil sky.

Cobalt Therapy Again Today

Cobalt therapy again today,
After the diagnostic technetate.
Shares in isotopes rise –
Her red count drops.
Her hair falls out – it
Was expected.

Nothing is expected of the treatment;
These are secondaries. She stays,
Too cheerful to bear for long,
With the priest.
She would have liked
To have seen a healer,

But this is resisted.
Gamma sources must have their turn.
Only when those fail
Will they re-label her,
Give her the glamour and nepenthe
Of terminal care.

On retreat, in the sandstone light
Of a Saxon chapel, we pray for her,
Taking the roof off our lives –
Letting her down inside us.
The intensity shocks.
We tremble as the rays hit.

Who then is holding whom
On the stretcher?
The door swings open
Between light and light.
We cannot look. She is too weak
To unfasten her shoes.

The many doors
Of our castles
Swing open in sympathy.
We are irradiated, room by room,
Our favourite cankers
Targets now.

We would rather have had the drugs.
We long for her to dance again.
We long for death, to take away the weight of glory.

Slipcatchers

Jane is ill enough now to be firmly labelled
Dying. We speak the forbidden word, but
Living would be more accurate
For every day has a different quality.

There are two boys. At their age
I fielded slip for a school eleven –
An alarming promotion. The space
Of possibility seemed vast, my arms leaden.

Now I am part of the care team
Who chatter at Jane, keeping up
Our spirits, and break off
To prognosticate for God.

We talk little now of healing.
The future is narrow-waisted,
We begin to look
Past the constriction.

The boys become our focus, and we
Unwilling slipcatchers
Poised in a cordon, waiting for them
To fly from the involuntary edge,

Uncertain if the deflection
Will be fine and fast, or slow, looping,
The grief hard to sight
Against the light
                         Of the forbidden city.

Very tender, with great stillness and serenity

The lived-out minutes, ground out into hours.
Intensive Care's neutral, functional seating.
Carrier-bags and travel-mugs.
Erratic drip-feed of information.
Clotting in the ventricles, cycles of sedation,
Cranial pressure, periods of hope.

You tell of touching his hand,
Your eyes dry, beyond the tears
That fell as early alleluias
Tell of touching the pain of God
And that when even touching and talking
Was forbidden

Love carried, carried.

Crying Freedom

*written after seeing the film 'Cry Freedom' on the day
two British soldiers were trapped in an IRA funeral*

The film primes opinions. Freedom
Is our cry. The long body, prone, brown,
Is Biko. The policemen are evil.
There is a plea in our hearts for pardon
For the complicitous six of Sharpeville.
We want the Afrikaaners to lose at power-tennis –
Their guns and riot-shields will not protect
For ever. In time they will go under.

The photograph, next morning, is of Ulster.
The body, no actor's, supine, bloody,
Is a British soldier's, torn
At a political funeral, like Biko's.
There is revenge in our hearts, against
Any who were in that riot. We want
Better shields, effective police. The SAS.

There is too much leisure for opinion
In our English flower-gardens.
Our hearts riot; the words in them
Tangle, like ornamental ivy –
Justice, lust, compassion, Barabbas.
We are at the worst station of the Cross –
The one at which we feel our reflexes fail.

Sestina for Karen and Ros and Sue, Richard and Peter and Simon, and many others

I came here when I was nineteen, to get well
from a kind of flash-flood of down, from a tyrant rule
of spiders over the thin moon of me. Safe from harm
here, they said. The film'll run slowly. Under control.
No-one will have to know. No-one will notice.
They didn't say I'd come out with a label.

Mind you, it was a kind of comfort, the label,
at first. People could see I'd fallen down a well
that was real. It made them take notice.
Then we lost our insurance. It's a rule,
the girl on the phone said. So I lost control
and broke the phone. My friend left. Only then the self-harm

and the Seclusion Room. What's the harm,
I said, if I cut myself? Is that the wrong label?
They tried things out till I was under control:
thirty milligrams the spiders. Seventy milligrams, well,
numbness, like living yesterday over. Fifty mgs rule
O.K. Not disruptive enough to notice.

I watch the trees a lot. I stand by the notice
That says all visitors must sign in and out. Harm-
less words. I tell another patient it's a good rule.
He tells me I'm a police spy. I like that label.
Whoever made my loneliness made it well.
But who was it? And is he still in control?

Sometimes I stand and think – this is a sick plan to control
a special person who's been fighting stuff a long time. 'Notice
the difference, when you treat me right!' I shout. Does no harm.
It *is* better here, than years ago. Same label –
but they ask about the colour of the bricks in your well.
Sometimes they help you choose to go ahead and keep a rule.

Maybe it has to be that certain drugs rule
your life, that without them there's just no control
over the downs. But staff *do* talk to you, go past the label,
if you get the right one, with some time to notice
you. To see you're choosing between living and no more harm
ever again. I read once that all shall be well –

tell me then: if I knew every rule, and could get people to notice
me, and was under control with the drugs, and was no harm
to anyone, and lost my label, would I be called well?

Carols at the Mental Hospital

A band of imported choirboys
fill the unfamiliar, locked-all-year air
with carols. Once in royal ...
The holly and ... the inevitable herald angels.

The singers tell the story that pure sound
can still transform musty space
into heaven. That there is still innocence
and possibility.

                    Also that some souls
are born under fortunate stars,
sing in cathedrals,
and get saxophones for Christmas.

Others are consigned
to dingy air
to sweat out memories
of their last Nowell.

Masters of roll-ups.
                    Abandoned of families.
Tellers of lifelines.
                    Stumblers over life.

The angels are diplomats, then,
silent in waiting
when the hard question comes
as to why.

They dance a heralds' dance –
now on that treble's mop of curls,
now on the bankrupt farmer
in the front row,
now on the snooker-player next door,
icily picking off red and black,
red and black,
his named nurse watching.

What they herald is holly, dark and sharp;
blood dried black on a crowned head;
the sun obscured and the star stood still;
and royal-red memories woven without seam –

rolled up, flung down, turned.

He went out to a deserted place

Deserted by love – familiar enough.
Love comes always erratically
to her assignations.

Deserted by goodness.
That is to have old suspicions confirmed.

Deserted by meaning. That
is the lifeless shelf of sand
surrounded by ocean, the dark thicket,
the address where even Job's God
is not at home, and prayer
disappears without trace. Once you find this place
it proves to be everywhere.

For C. N.

Even a maple leaf
Drifting down sunlight
Into a muddy creek
Hits the brown water with a flash.

How much more
Must a dying saint of God
Colliding with heaven
Flood the eyes that see.

Funeral Wind

It was warm, for January, in a church
packed with overcoats paying their respects.
Dignitaries outdid themselves to search
for tributes – he had mastered many dialects
of learning, had taught the great, saw into the grain
of living, understood mystics, knew others' pain.

He passed, in a plain box, out the South Door.
Children he'd loved had gathered there
awkwardly, as though still looking for more
of his smile. In the West Tower
the bells hung silent. The wind, fierce from the north,
had no such scruple. It gave a cold greeting to death,

buffeting the beaten trees in the churchyard,
the small party at the graveside. So hard
to concentrate on the last prayers – heart willing,
shoulders hunched at the cold. A killing
by cancer. A large spirit quenched. Tired earth
sheltered alone from an ill wind's mirth.

Bearing Reality – for Silke Bischof

*Silke Bischof was taken hostage by bank-robbers in August
1988, and appeared in numerous (posed) pictures in the
media. She was shot during a police ambush. She was 18.*

Step out of role, Silke, don't you go
Playing with men with big guns again.
We cannot bear much of you and him –
Not with our breakfast things – cereal
Just does not go with undiluted
Fear. We would like to be directors –
Call for a cut and hand you cashmere
Sweaters and smiles, and say no more takes
Like that one, Silke dear, you were just
Brilliant. Eyes held the right stillness –
Death in them. I liked the hair, which you
Couldn't brush back – Dieter's gun hand stopped you
(Only his thumb on the hammer kept
You alive – very good, that last touch) –
Your lower lip starting to go forward,
Sobs coming but for now unstated.
Cut of near genius, we'd tell each other,
Safe in the canteen, and you'd smile and shrug.

You are a still, Silke, unsmiling.
We will see gun hand and eyes, lips,
Fair, girlish hair for a long long time
After we throw the newspaper out.
We'll all the while yearn to run the film
On, to find somewhere in your last hours
Quality, richness of life, even
God perhaps. Nothing presents itself.

No smile. Not even the arched-shouldered
Scream behind that look of steady fear.
Press work gets better and better of course –
Shot good of Dieter, binoculars,
Leather and hammer-clawing hand –
Photographer got all that, and you did not
Turn your head once – at the ambush made
Just enough space to be shot in the heart,
Leaving us that quite still, lovely,
Aspirationless face, remembered

Long past your name, and our
Thousandth debate about evil.

PART FIVE

Longings and Destinations

The Mosaicist

When I was younger I would sometimes boast
In gold, and calculate a grand design.
Now I know I lack that taint, the almost-
Madness of creation, the genius of line.
I colour others' angels, attempt again
The sturdy Tree of Life – consistency
Of halo, hart, and heav'n, technique leaf-thin,
In these must be my petty mastery.
And they have made me teacher now, among
The shining stones, discerner of early talents;
My self-denial, the smile I give the young
As mists of colour stir, is read as balance.
The Lord alone knows patience for a liar
And how I long to see these dusts take fire.

Holly Leaf

for Sandy (written after the suppression of the Tiananmen
Square protests)

You find for me a holly leaf, last year's,
Reduced by time to a fine skein, an outline
In brittle thread of what had shone with green
Last June. So it is with my faith too, although
I do not show such doubt, but promise you
An Incarnation-poem from the leaf
That sits so obstinate upon my desk.

I do not know if it is nurture, patience,
Or His long, terrifying suffering of us
That lets elaborate construct fade,
Unseenness stay, as we think on God.
In China they are rounding up the free –
Their future suddenly brittle, faded.

And so I write about a thing which, mainly
Space and silence, still retains the outline
Of a tiny crown of thorns, and whispers too
Of Christmas. Holly we believe
Is evergreen, and evil not as strong
As good. Counter-example tears the weft –
But what persists is fine, beyond evaluing.

Kinds of Faith

You ask – if I can see the green
In this long swoop of fields

Down off the moor, as we pick our way
By moonlight. I say we can't – I say

We infer the colour, that that is part
Of the beauty. What stretches the heart

Has in fact the hue of settled snow.
But you say, having waited, and heard, no:

We *can* be definite – though the dance
Of space, hedged, arranged, is at the last

Limit of our sense, the retina
Retains the green. The shared blear

Of snowlight sweeps to the scarp's edge.
We can agree, at least, that glory follows death.

My soul like a weaned child

the first verse is a quotation from Psalm 131

'I do not occupy myself with things
too great and marvellous for me.
But I have calmed and quieted my soul
like a weaned child with its mother;
my soul is like the weaned child that is with me.'

My soul like a weaned child
sometimes held to me in such a bliss
of light on childish skin
as my soul takes her ease
at the edge of sleep
that on those days I have to watch only
in case some extravagant dream
float the infant so far
over cliffs of gold
that I cannot retrieve her from glory.

There are other days. They are characterised
by a racket of complaint –
if not actual food-flinging.

Destination

I use the moor today, ashamedly,
as an antidote
to blind family anger.

I start the long slope of Hameldown
(the far ridge like a line
of scripture, forbidding self-love).

Wind against. A white film dusting
the kists. Deer-sprites
seem to haunt the valley-floors.

The sky is empty, wash-blue, as though
some controlled explosion
had cleared away its debris

leaving only light, and three thorn
trees, absolute
as to sharpness. Suffering.

The snow's striations are intricate,
seem hand-turned;
melt-pools dissolve my eyes.

I find rest in hard ascent, my chaos
left printed in the white,
false summits disregarded.

As I stump down off the hill the snow
drifts after me, erasing
my working. I walk away empty –

begin again today, apparently,
but feel somehow foreknown,
like that new-etched scimitar of moon.

Leaning on the Spring – a prayer

Leaning out along a beech-branch
High above a quick-flowing river
I watch the buds mottle and fatten
Towards leaf-point
And spread my weight out
For what seems like the first time in years,
Spread out my weight onto the gathering spring.

For years now hope
Has been quickly followed by disaster
And I have learned to furl it close.

Uncurl it, Lord, this Eastertide –
I know the water's transience
And yet the sunlight makes on it
A standing jigsaw
Bright as filigreed silver.
I know the hurt of many memories
And yet when swimming collies
Shatter the bright pattern of the Esk
My doubting will gladdens,
My knotted heart stretches towards healing.

Unfurl, I pray, my trust again.

Eight Steps and an Arch

Epithalamion

A tunnelled lane,
              alley for sparrowhawks.
A light and open place,
              caucus of friends at every age and stage.
All is ribboned and ready,
              for hand-fasting.
She will have the first drink from his cup.
              He will be the wine in her cup.
She will be the shield for his back.
              He will be shield upon her breast.
There will be fury, but never slander,
              deep breaths, caught breaths,
Tears, surprised in the fearless,
              many sonnets.
Music, recalling lanterns on a long-ago river,
              more joy than one heart can handle.
High-arching peace from the Prince of Peace to you,
              love-woven, guarding.

Masaccio's Eve

from the fresco of 'The Expulsion from the Garden' in the
Cappella Brancacci, Santa Maria del Carmine, Florence

Adam's distress we recognise;
It is a strong minor chord for all instruments –
Sustained, grieving, not looking at even
The possibility of modulation,
But all of a weave with itself.
Perhaps it is that in his heart
He is able to blame the woman
While still accepting his own victimhood.

For Eve young Masaccio – early twenties,
Hardly launched on his career –
Has found a note of far vaster desolation.
Or not one note exactly, but all the notes that come
When bows are drawn slowly across strings
Held away into dissonance.
So slow the drawing that every unevenness in the surface
Of each bow sets up its own grating.

It is in her body, yes, and in the unfeeling
Clasp of hands to breasts and groin –
Hands that deny there can ever again be bodily joy.
But most of all the torment is in the eyes –
Auschwitz eyes – five hundred years too early.
How does a Masaccio, a Mozart,
Make that move, start such dissonance
Running, as stretches spirits to new spaces of strain?
Who is the other who walks so close

into the unfamiliar land?

From Annigoni's 'Joseph' in San Lorenzo, Florence

A plank
is a stairway
is a hammer
is a cross.

A man
is a treetrunk
is an artist
is a father, blessing.

The child
receives the sunlight
the scripture
the love.

For now the workshop is the world
is like a second skin to them both.

Where cloud intrudes,
it is flat, blood-red.

Two Maquettes

I am a rock, when work requires it.
Those expecting a hard surface
encounter one.

Anyone who probes at all further,
using a special drill
or a gentle question,

strikes different grain, broken, faulted,
strikes anxiety,
unprocessed pain.

Below that, sunlit, elusive memories
free-floating on a sea of grief.

* * * * * *

I am a block of faulted marble
which a sculptor
touches with hands

more knowing than any lover's,
seeking to release
a masterpiece. He calls it

'Human Being Fully Alive'.
Even experts dispute
the extent of his handiwork

in the unfinished study of me
people call 'The Captive'.

Preaching Easter

Last meeting of the carers' group.
All were asked to bring
a symbol, an object to hold up
to show what the group
had *meant* to us.
Half had forgotten, but all,
dutifully, wrenched something
out of pocket or bag
and spoke on it.

Preachers, no less than the rest,
become wrenchers
of symbols, asserting things
of wood, wine, water and light
very near to lies

and all the time we
are wrenched by symbols
we shall never speak about –
those we almost managed to love,
and through the space of almost
have never understood, thinking
them wood, or wine,
water, or light –

those whom we have seen tear
the weft of life, doing it violence,
doing wrong we have colluded with
and fail to call
nails, or gall, or night.

Easter morning is the most outrageous
wrench of all, doing death violence,
ruining the space of almost.
It is as though God,
waiting his turn in the circle,
had given *his* answer,
dragging it up from somewhere –
some source of splinters, yeasts, floods,
and floods of light.

Doing Church

is like handling an exquisite, fantastic phial
made of smoked glass. Inside
a mysterious oil that might be gladness,
or glory, or myrrh. We toss it from hand to hand
                              or in the old model
we watch a priest juggle it.

On a bad day no-one sees the smoked swirls
of vermilion and indigo.
On a bad day everything works, or nothing works,
but nothing hints, nothing glistens.

On a good day
a held silence, a shared smile,
light fires occasional oil-drops
that flash like silver, or white gold.
                              All too seldom
the glass smashes, floods the air
with the scent of heaven. Soon enough gone.
Always another Sunday. A new mystery
in smoked glass.

Sunset over Exmoor

From the Crown Hotel, Exford,
Where they still have stabling for gentlemen,
We watch the sunset by dint
Of discount vouchers. There almost had
To be a poem there, to justify the bill.
Privilege. Poetry at several pounds a line.

Is it accountability, then,
That draws from me
How those clouds lie
On that western hill
Like quill pens,
Their feather-edges honed
As the sun falls away from them,
Gone to boil the sea beyond Lynmouth?

Or is it love
That gives me eyes and words?
The deer think their way
Up onto the hill, beside the sky,
That same love's
Most generous calligraphy.

The Reunion

We assemble, in the long library,
The scent in the beeswax of the polish
Of which is precisely unchanged, and
Exchange, over dinner, surfaces,
Contrasted marriages and careers;
While we are sober we do not look
Too near the grain
For fear of harsher weathering.

The solicitors have worn dark and safe, their secrets
Locked in boxes lettered white on black.
The bankers have taken a high veneer;
They bellow bond-issues at each other,
Point out honours on boards,
Put down sons on ten-year plans.
The doctors' eyes have seen fifteen years'
Pain, and have not come to discuss it.

I recognise only the face of the engraver,
The gouger of glowing copper. There
I see ravages – seams of work worn out,
New workings, going deeper
For deeper ore.
His work has taught him time –
The shortness of it, the disciplined
Desperation of working in a corroding
Medium, with hands that will not
Always be steady, the challenge of the virgin
Surface, so easily sinned on.

We are drunk now, flushed
With the wine that used to be forbidden.
We talk, arthritis, debt,
And thirty-year sentences –
Terms of mediocrity.
We are etched, all of us,
Unvirgin, imprecise alloys,
By the royal acid of the will of God.

But for Morning Chapel,
Tomorrow, at eleven,
Our masks will be safely on.

The Fourth Plinth

the Fourth Plinth programme, now the responsibility of the Mayor of London, commissions various works to fill the vacant plinth in Trafalgar Square

The current competitors are a six-storey windmill,
five mirrors,
four meerkats,
a three-masted ship in a bottle,
a burned-out car (two-door)
and an empty space protected by a net.

I claim   all four plinths
for what I would want   always to remember.

On the first I place
the thorn-crowned man,
a young Jewish kingdom-prophet.
London dwarfs him. He
eclipses it.

On the second two holograms
of your face as we wake –
one to hold your loveliness,
one to track the surprise across your eyes
as you remember
how hard and long we have loved.

On the third I place
my three best teachers –
a scientist, a priest and a poet,
absolute in their integrity, their lives
asymptotic to compromise.

The fourth is harder, I concede.
I place on it
the light on the Wallabrook, the breeze off Hawaii,
and the Skye wind beating up out of Cor'Uisg.
My last talk with my mother.
Scraps of the Times Crossword, uncompleted.

Nudes by Titian and Modigliani,
surge of Beethoven seven,
the high Sierra from Half-Dome,
and a mating combination
for knights at chess.

I reserve the right to change this provision at sunset.
I bring in how the lead lights rattled
in my grandmother's door as it opened,
how a leopard moves through long grass,
my son driving the green at the fourteenth,
and the whole Appalachian Trail, in fall colour.

To save space, and in the interests of economy,
the whole of Bach, Plato and T. S. Eliot
are available on an iPod,
neatly placed between the transeptal towers
of Exeter Cathedral.

There are some more private moments.
I show these in the darkness
with Trafalgar Square cordoned off
and the lions hooded, for modesty.
The actors know their parts.
We dance them without rehearsal or regret.

Only my request for the whole city of Venice
on a fine sharp day in winter
has caused the Mayor concern.
Health and Safety are afraid I may take a chill, and sue,
and so bump up the congestion charge.

Mozart's Requiem in a Village Church

There is some trepidation
In the rural strings
And more in the audience

As they shuffle in, cope
With pillars. Some, well-briefed,
Whisper of Süssmayr.

We begin. The bassoonist, punk, twenty,
Down from London by one-two-five,
Is easy with her part;

Her counterpoint is light –
She is not foxed by Bax
Or ruffled by Duruflé,

But as she plays I see
Her heart fall, Constanze's,
Into the scoring,

Our hearts, alto quavers,
Plaintive bird-cries,
Are overstridden in the bass –

We are all alone
With mortality
And the *Agnus Dei*.

At last the Requiem
Dies away into
Rook-broken quietness.

Punk and pensioner rest
A moment, at the lych-gate,
Brought together by a death.

Village Funerals

Fifteen years ago
I would have looked at myself
attending, *dulce et decorum*,
admired the grave style
with which I sat my pew,
and sang the sad hymns.

In fifteen more years
I'll be leaning
hard on the woodwork,
with the fixity of stare
my parents use
to look into death's approach.

So these are the good years,
when I grieve as much
for the old village, contemplating
depletion, as for myself, and call
my presence solidarity
rather than form, rather than anguish.

The Woodworker and the Poet

for Bill Hooper

We stood before the Christmas crib, the church's
Proud acquisition – you I knew had made
The frame, had sanded, stained, jointed it –
And what, you asked, what does a poet do?
A maker, I said – knee-jerk answer,
Schoolboy Greek – a poet is a maker.

I wanted all the time to run my hand
Across the finely-finished wood – you watched me
Want that, your gift securely jointed to life:
Words are precarious, dishonoured,
Their making a high conceit for humans, as is
Affecting to see into the grain of things.

Think of the power of words, I said, to make
Great lies. Strip them out – shape them new –
That is the poet's chore. You smiled, and I,
Relieved to satisfy you, turned to the holy scene.
A chance, for once, at strong-jointed joy –
Your making, humble, full of honest doubt,

Houses the saving word.

Beethoven Quartet Op. 132; T. S. Eliot, 'East Coker'

from the celebration of the 50th anniversary of the interment of Eliot's ashes in St Michael's, East Coker, 26 September 2015

A state of readiness slows the air
until at last, chord by wistful chord, music
sets the molecules of the church in order,
unrushed, unclotted, striving through time
to resolution. We are released from prayer
into wonder, into longed-for space.

In a brief interval, minds dally with the space.
We watch it rearrange itself, the air
recollecting centuries given to prayer –
its rigour, its silence, its music,
the way it transmutes time.
Then the poem calls us to order.

Word by word, words in turn re-order,
craft, crystallise the space.
The poem fashions silence, attends to time,
hallows it, makes it ordinary in this blent air,
gives it pulse, slows the wandering music
in our minds, makes its contrapuntal prayer.

We are not required to invest in prayer.
We are implored to stay in these moments, in order
that our all-too-unequal music
can take leave of this space,
stream out into the Indian summer air
with less need to snatch at time.

We have been quiet here, for a time,
with bitter old Beethoven, whose prayer
for hearing will be answered only in the air
of heaven. With Mr Eliot, who in order
to make poetry, suffered and betrayed. This space
pardons him, and us. But what music

can we take away, what possible music
can hold this meaning for us? Time
sweeps it away, disperses it across space.
Not even Cranmer's Common Prayer
can clutch it back, set it in order.
But something goes with us, out into the evening air.

It is not music, for that requires time.
It is a feeling of outline, of order to air,
a space of peace and grace, beyond what prayer
can pray for.

Prayer

'Lord thou knowest that I am growing older
And will soon be old.'
Scarlet is more elusive now
And I do not miss it
As I think I ought.
Gold drips through my life still
Paler than I remembered.
I am trapped here with a mass of blue –
I stare into it, begin to notice
What a range it has – pallid enough
To allow clarity that disturbs
Deep enough to shut out
All but the smallest hint of light.

Blue is the colour I need to learn
The blue of the young Mary's robe
As she speaks before she thinks
Be it unto me.
               Standing there between soldiers,
Hired hands in red and gold. Standing there
Keening, comforted only by the friends
Who had failed him.
                     The sudden singing blue
Of seeing him again.
                    Violet-flecked black
Of her own death, which yet will mean
Always seeing him, beyond all possible gold.

Acknowledgements

Versions of some of the poems have appeared in: *Ars Interpres*, *Christian*, *Crucible*, *Encounter*, *Envoi*, *Fire*, *Interpreter's House*, *Landscape or Land?*, *Otter*, *Outposts*, *Paris Atlantic*, *Sepia*, *Spiritus*, *The Collins Anthology of Contemporary Christian Poetry*, *The Exeter Book of Riddles*, *The Lamp-Post*, *The West Branch*, *Third Way*, *Yellow Crane*.

'Three Deserted Wives' was highly commended in the South-West Poetry Competition, and read on Radio 3 at Choral Evensong for Epiphany.

'Coming to Terms' was read on Radio 4 as part of the programme 'Something Understood'.

'Patmos' was nominated for a Pushcart Prize.

I warmly thank my editor at Shoestring Press, John Lucas, for permission to reproduce poems from the following collections: *Beyond the Bitter Wind*, *Easing the Gravity Field: poems of science and love*, *A Gash in the Darkness*, and *Chasing the Raven*.

Some of these poems were written during a Hawthornden Fellowship, and I thank the Trustees for their support. I am also grateful to the centre 'Waves of Three Seas' on the island of Rhodes for a very generative stay there in 2001.

'Rendering Voices' was commissioned by the Nida Institute for Biblical Scholarship at the American Bible Society, in collaboration with the Society of Biblical Literature, for presentation at the International Meeting of the Society of Biblical Literature at King's College London, July 2011.

'Sestina for Karen ...' was commissioned by the local NHS Trust to express the concerns of long-term sufferers of mental illness, and read in the Service held in Exeter Cathedral to mark 50 years of the NHS in Devon.